THATC

Patterns of Deceit

By the same author

ONE MAN'S FALKLANDS

THATCHER'S TORPEDO: THE SINKING OF THE 'BELGRANO'

THATCHER:
Patterns of Deceit

Tam Dalyell
Introduction by Paul Rogers

CECIL WOOLF·LONDON

First published 1986
©1986 Tam Dalyell; Introduction © 1986 Paul Rogers

Cecil Woolf Publishers, 1 Mornington Place, London NW1 7RP
Tel: 01-387 2394

ISBN 0-900821-87-6 hardback edition
ISBN 0-900821-86-8 paperback edition

Contents

CONTENTS

Introduction
Conduct Unbecoming

On 6 June 1986, the Labour MP Tam Dalyell was prevented from speaking in the House of Commons by a Government-organised filibuster. It was the latest move in a long controversy originating with his opposition to the Falklands War.

Under the British parliamentary system, a back-bench MP has several means of pursuing the government of the day on an issue of substance. The parliamentary question, whether written or oral, is the most common method, but skill and persistence are usually required as ministers and civil servants are well versed in avoiding direct answers.

Speeches in regular debates are also useful but an even more effective way of illuminating an issue is for an MP to instigate his own debate. Opportunities for this are rare as MPs have to ballot for the right to raise a subject of their choice on one of just six Fridays in each parliamentary year.

By early 1986, Tam Dalyell had been an MP for over twenty years but had never succeeded in even being in the top twenty in this lottery. When the result of the 1986 ballot was announced to the House of Commons on 21 May, in his presence, he had the usual remote chance.

This time, however, he was successful and the result was greeted with hearty approval from the Labour benches and some ribald laughter from the Conservative side. It induced a look of benign resignation from the Leader of

the House, John Biffen, and a distinct *sotto voce* expletive
from an unidentified Member of the Government Front
Bench, 'Oh, Heavens no, not *him*!'

Tam Dalyell announced his topic then and there: 'I beg
to give notice that I shall raise the subject of my concern
at the behaviour of the Prime Minister in relation to Westlands, the sending of F1-11s to Libya, and the Falklands
War', this occasioning more support from Labour and
Alliance Benches and groans from the Conservatives.

Over the next few days he took advice from his Labour
colleagues on whether to use the occasion to mount a full-
scale attack on the behaviour of the Prime Minister on these
issues, what would amount to a motion of censure. There
were strong arguments against this. Firstly, Friday is not a
Party day but a House of Commons day, and a censure
motion is normally the province of the Leader of the Opposition. Secondly, an offensive motion would unnecessarily
antagonise those increasing numbers of Conservative MPs
becoming critical of the leadership, style and behaviour of
the Prime Minister on the issues in question. Finally, the
aim of the debate was primarily to seek information concerning her conduct. Censure would certainly rule this out.

Thus a motion was formulated:

Conduct of the Prime Minister
Mr Tam Dalyell
To call attention to the conduct of the Prime Minister in
relation to Westlands, the sending of F1-11 aircraft to
Libya, the Falklands War; and to move, That this House
invites the Prime Minister to explain in detail her role in
the Westlands affair and the decision to leak selectively
a law officer's letter to a Minister of the Crown; to
present, in relation to the United States attack on Libya,
the evidence relating to the safest means of achieving
particular objectives with the lowest possible risk both of

civilian casualties in Libya and casualties among United States service personnel, on the basis of which she allowed President Reagan to use bases in the United Kingdom for the F1-11 raids on Libya, and to answer, point by point, the questions addressed to her about her conduct in relation to the Falklands War by the honourable Members for Bow and Poplar, Newham South, Falkirk West and Doncaster North, printed in the Minutes of Proceedings of the Foreign Affairs Committee of 16 July 1985.

The last week in May 1986 was the Whit Recess, with Tam Dalyell starting work on his speech, intending it to be a means of getting a direct response from the Government on the many controversial aspects of the three events. Within days, though, it became clear that the Government was growing concerned about the opportunity he would have to present his arguments. While his persistent criticisms of Government policy over the Falklands had initially been written off by Conservatives as the preoccupation of a crank, the events of 1984, with copious leaks about the *Belgrano* and the arrest of Clive Ponting, had made him a much more formidable opponent. On 1 June, *The Sunday Times* carried a report that the Government had deliberately scheduled a debate on the Channel Tunnel for the evening before Tam Dalyell's debate. The Channel Tunnel debate would be sufficiently open-ended for a filibuster to be mounted by Conservative back-benchers which could run through the night and beyond 9.30am on the Friday. That day's business would then be lost and Tam Dalyell prevented from initiating his debate.

The newspaper also reported what amounted to a belt-and-braces move by the Government Whips, who put a three-line whip on Friday's business, just in case it did go ahead as scheduled, in order to ensure a massive Government presence and a majority in any vote. Dalyell followed up *The Sunday*

Times' report and found that it had originated not in the
Whips' office but in Downing Street, but, even as late as the
day before the debate Dalyell and other Labour MPs
doubted that the Government would actually pursue their
intent to sabotage his debate. Eradicating parliamentary
time allocated to Private Members is not unknown, but it is
seldom wise for a Government to be seen to indulge in it
and several Conservative MPs voiced their disagreement with
the tactic at a 1922 Committee meeting on the Thursday
night.

In the event, some fourteen Conservative back-benchers
contrived to keep the Channel Tunnel debate going through
the night, but by early morning the filibuster attempt to
silence Dalyell was already gaining far greater press coverage
than the debate itself. In due course, and to quote *The Times*:

> Mr Dalyell arrived in the Commons at 9 am to find
> progress on the Bill still under way. Debate on the Chan-
> nel Tunnel Bill ended at 9.17 am but an adjournment
> debate ensured that proceedings on Thursday's business
> were kept going until after 9.30 am at which time Mr
> Dalyell's Friday motion fell. The House rose at 9.47am.

Reaction from both sides of the House was swift. For
Labour, Peter Shore described it as a 'disgraceful and
squalid manoeuvre', and the Conservative back-bencher,
Robert Rhodes James said, 'This was a squalid shambles
and a disgrace to the Government and to the Conservative
Party. Someone must explain this deliberate, calculated
cheating. I gather there are moves to call the Chief Whip
to appear before the 1922 to do some explaining. . . . I
have yet to meet a Tory MP who is not absolutely enraged
at the folly of it all.' He could not understand how those
Conservative MPs who had vigorously defended freedom of
speech in the universities could explain to their constituents

their participation in the debate. Certainly the filibuster
tactic had the opposite effect to that intended. Tam Dalyell
proceeded to deliver his speech in a Committee Room at
the House to journalists and fellow Labour MPs and the
affair dominated the news for the rest of the day. Most
commentators concluded that the Government had contrived yet another banana skin, not least when it was
revealed that the Prime Minister herself had approved the
filibuster tactic.

In one sense, though, the tactic succeeded, in that media
attention concentrated on the apparent censoring of an MP
rather than the content of the arguments he had intended
to present, and this is the main reason for publishing the
speech here for a wider readership. Behind this, though, is
the leading question: why did the Government believe it so
necessary to silence Tam Dalyell? Why, indeed, was the
Prime Minister herself sympathetic to the methods used
when they appeared to amount to a disregard for the
procedures of the House? Just what did the Government
fear from Tam Dalyell?

To attempt to answer this, we need to go back briefly to
the origins of Tam Dalyell's campaign on the conduct of
the Prime Minister, back to the Falklands War itself.

*   *   *   *   *   *

When Argentina invaded the Falkland Islands in April 1982,
Tam Dalyell was one of a minority of Labour MPs who
believed that the despatch of the Task Force was a dangerous
over-reaction which could well lead to a bloody conflict.
So strong did his opposition become during the course of
the war that he was sacked by Michael Foot from his position
of Shadow Minister of Science, which he had held since
1980.

In the whole Falklands War, the weekend of 1-2 May 1982
was regarded as pivotal. By that time, major elements of the

Task Force had arrived in the vicinity of the islands, the US mediation effort of Al Haig had come to an end to be replaced by US support for Britain, and intensive peace negotiations were being attempted by both Peru and the United Nations.

Up to 1 May no British serviceman had been killed by Argentine military action, yet on that day, elements of the Task Force embarked on a series of raids on the Stanley Air Base and Goose Green which used dedicated anti-personnel munitions and caused considerable loss of life on the Argentine side. On Sunday, 2 May the 43-year-old Argentine cruiser *General Belgrano* was sunk with the loss of 368 lives by the submarine *HMS Conqueror*. The war escalated rapidly and two days later *HMS Sheffield* was lost.

In the two years following the war, Tam Dalyell became convinced that the UK Government had decided that a military solution to the conflict was domestically essential if the Government was to survive: a negotiated settlement would raise far too great a controversy concerning the Government's failure to prevent the initial Argentine invasion. He further became convinced that the *Belgrano* had been torpedoed, on orders from Chequers, when the Prime Minister was already aware of a major Peruvian peace initiative. In effect he believed that the *Belgrano* incident had torpedoed a diplomatic settlement and that this outcome was intended.

While he relied on leaks from several well-informed sources for this particular conclusion, a combination of other leaks and the results of a remarkable and sustained campaign of hundreds of parliamentary questions certainly showed that the original Government account of the circumstances surrounding the sinking of the cruiser was almost entirely false. His four main parliamentary speeches on the subject were subsequently published under the title *Thatcher's Torpedo* (Cecil Woolf, 1983). The Government had declared that the *Belgrano* was attacked as soon as it was located, that the Captain of the *Conqueror* acted on his own initiative and that the *Belgrano* was heading into the Total Exclusion Zone which Britain had declared around the Falkland Islands. Tam Dalyell was eventually able to establish that the *Belgrano* had actually been tracked by *Conqueror* for over 30 hours before being attacked, that orders for the attack came direct from London, and that the cruiser had been heading *away* from the Total Exclusion Zone and *away* from the Task Force for the eleven hours leading up to the time she was sunk.

Over the initial two years of his campaign Tam Dalyell was ridiculed by Government and many sections of the media. He took his evidence to scores of public meetings throughout the country, often attracting many hundreds of people to hear him speak. By early 1984 sufficient evidence had accumulated to convince many people that there must be something in his claims. This, in turn, persuaded Labour members of the House of Commons Foreign Affairs Select Committee to press for answers to certain key questions concerning diplomatic initiatives over the Falklands War.

The Government response was to mislead the Committee, but this was revealed to Tam Dalyell by a leak from within the Ministry of Defence, an event leading to the arrest of Clive Ponting in mid-July 1984. Immediately after Mr Ponting's arrest, the full details of this deception were released, not incidentally by Tam Dalyell, to *The Observer* and the *New Statesman*. At the same time, and from another source, the *New Statesman* was informed that during the Falklands War the UK Government had despatched a Polaris missile submarine to the South Atlantic as a back-up in the event of a disaster affecting the Task Force. Thus the Government was so concerned to ensure a military victory that it was prepared to threaten the use of nuclear weapons against Argentina, a non-nuclear power.

Early in 1985, Clive Ponting was tried and acquitted at
the Old Bailey of charges under Section 2 of the Official
Secrets Act. Meanwhile, the Foreign Affairs Select Committee, prompted by the apparent deception practised by
the Ministry of Defence, pursued a detailed investigation of
the events of 1-2 May 1982.

During the early part of 1985, the Committee split along
party lines, with the four Labour members conducting what
was, in effect, their own investigation. As a result, the Committee eventually delivered majority and minority reports.
The majority, Conservative, report, while somewhat critical
of the Government on its handling of information about
the events concerned, exonerated the Government of the
charges levelled over the previous three years by Tam
Dalyell. Labour's minority report ran to over 30,000 words
and ended with 30 questions which it requested the Government to answer. It was deeply critical of much of the
Government's behaviour and remains the most comprehensive
indictment yet formulated, a remarkable and detailed
critique of Government action both before and during the
war.

Unusually, the report was not published until right at
the end of the parliamentary session, on 22 July 1985. By
what may not have been a coincidence, it was published
about an hour after the Popplewell Report into the tragic
fire at Bradford City Football Ground earlier that year. The
latter report dominated the media for the next twenty-four
hours. Most unusually for such a major foreign affairs report,
the Government did not provide time for the usual Commons debate. Indeed, the Government's only official
response was a six-page document published four months
later. The Foreign Affairs Committee report costs £12.00
and the Government's response a further £1.35. Sales
have not been high.

Tam Dalyell's speech on 6 June this year was, in part, an

attempt to focus on those unanswered questions put by
the four Labour members of the Select Committee:

1. At what date and on what grounds did the War Cabinet abandon its prime purpose of deploying and using
   military action in support of diplomatic initiative and
   economic pressure for a negotiated settlement and
   change to a 'miliatry solution' as the main criterion
   for action?
2. In addition to official communications, what information, if any, about the Peruvian peace initiative did
   the Prime Minister or other Ministers receive from
   other sources, including the United States Embassy in
   Lima, or sources in Britain or elsewhere?
3. What intercepts were made, and when, of orders to the
   Argentine fleet; which of them were decoded, and when;
   which of the decrypts were passed to Northwood, and
   when; and which were then passed to the War Cabinet,
   and when? Were the *Guardian* and *Observer* reports [5
   January 1985 and 6 January 1985, respectively] on
   this matter correct?

If answered in full, these questions would throw direct
light on Tam Dalyell's central claim, that the Prime Minister
ordered the sinking of the *Belgrano* in the full knowledge
of the Peruvian peace initiative, indeed that the Prime Minister and the War Cabinet deliberately sought war when a
negotiated settlement was possible.

*   *   *   *   *   *

In his questioning of the Government on the conduct of
the Falklands War and the post-war presentation of that
conduct, Tam Dalyell has repeatedly alleged a lack of
integrity. That too is a central feature of the other major
aspects of his speech, the US raid on Libya in April 1986

which involved UK-based F1-11s, and the Government
handling of the Westland affair.

There is one key feature in each event. For the F1-11
raid, it concerns the constant assertion by the Prime Minister that the F1-11 bombers were militarily essential for
the raid on Tripoli because of the nature of their capabilities,
particularly in relation to accurate delivery of munitions to
minimise 'collateral damage', a euphemism for civilian
casualties.

The US air strike on targets in Libya on 14-15 April was
the culmination of increasing antagonism to the Libyan
régime following a range of terrorist attacks in the Middle
East and Europe. Few European governments believed that
Libya was the most important source of terrorist action
and there was widespread opposition to the United States
mounting a major attack. Even so, the Reagan administration
believed that a show of force was required and ordered an
air strike which involved aircraft operating from carriers in
the Mediterranean and from bases in Britain.

The attack caused considerable civilian casualties and was
strongly criticised by the Opposition Parties in Britain.
Nationally there was also strong opposition to the use of US
bases in Britain, as there had been an almost universal
assumption that they were to be used solely in a NATO
role connected with the defence of Western Europe against
the Warsaw Pact. To counter this opposition to her
support for the United States, Mrs Thatcher sought to
insist on the military necessity for using the F1-11s from
Britain in order to carry out the attack.

By careful and precise reference to reports in the US
specialist press, especially the leading defence journal
Aviation Week and Space Technology, Tam Dalyell shows
otherwise. Inter-service rivalry (the US Air Force wanting
'a piece of the action'), a good training opportunity, a
chance to test out F1-11s over a long distance, and the

need to show that the US had at least one ally—these were certainly all good reasons. Strict military necessity was another matter altogether, for the aircraft carriers had the means to conduct the entire operation without aid from the F1-11s in Britain. Once again, Mr Dalyell's challenge relates to the Prime Minister's integrity when responding to questions on the subject in the House.

Then, finally, there is the Westland affair. This developed in the latter part of 1985 as the Westland Aircraft company slid into serious financial difficulties. There were two possible solutions, each involving foreign interests with which Westland already co-operated. The then Defence Secretary, Michael Heseltine, favoured Westland going in with a European consortium including West German and Italian companies, but others in Government, including the Prime Minister, favoured collaboration with the giant US helicopter corporation Sikorsky.

Mr Heseltine was heavily committed to the European option but by early 1986 he was increasingly fighting a rear-guard action, especially as the Westland board itself was in favour of the US option. He made several public statements in support of the European option, some of which may have had dubious legality. A result of this was that a senior Law Officer, the Solicitor-General, wrote a confidential letter to Mr Heseltine sections of which could be interpreted as being critical of his actions.

In a quite remarkable development, the letter was selectively leaked to the Press Association in a manner calculated to be damaging to the increasingly maverick Mr Heseltine. Shortly afterwards he resigned and in the subsequent controversy, Opposition politicians argued that the Prime Minister *must* have had knowledge of the decision to leak the Solicitor-General's letter to Mr Heseltine, once a copy of it had been received by Downing Street.

In perhaps the central feature of his speech, Tam Dalyell

produces new evidence to suggest that this attack missed the point. He states that the Solicitor-General was prompted to write the letter by Downing Street with the express purpose of its contents subsequently being leaked. The Solicitor-General would not, of course, be aware of, or a party to, this plan. Tam Dalyell provides precise details of how he came upon this information. He would claim that it is once again a matter of integrity of Government and Prime Minister.

*   *   *   *   *   *

We are left with one puzzling question. Just why did elements in the Government go to such extraordinary lengths to prevent Tam Dalyell making his speech on Friday, 6 June? Certainly he had become a thorn in the flesh of Government. Without doubt his claims concerning the conduct of the Falklands War had become increasingly credible, especially in the light of the Ponting affair. Yet most Conservative MPs had continued to treat him as a crank, and while his long campaign had damaged the Government, the wounds were hardly mortal.

It could be argued that, in the first few months of 1986, the Government had experienced an unusual sequence of difficulties and was decidedly jittery. Yet the massive majority remained and in the ordinary way Tam Dalyell's speech would have attracted little media attention.

At the same time, though, there is a quality and determination in his campaigning which is unnerving to government. During the past four years of harrying over the *Belgrano* incident, there have been many occasions when it has seemed that the controversy has finally sunk gracefully beneath the waves, only to surface when least expected. A leak here, an injudiciously answered parliamentary question there, or perhaps even a missing log book — all add up to more embarrassment. Perhaps a government with things to hide is always worried by a tenacious back-bencher.

In the days before the aborted speech, three different matters may have been of concern to the Government. The first was the original question of Government knowledge of the Peruvian peace plan during the Falklands War. Bearing in mind the categorical denial of knowledge of the Peruvian plan oft-repeated by Ministers and indeed the Prime Minister, if Tam Dalyell had finally managed to gain evidence to the contrary, then the Government would have been in serious trouble. One might succeed in the dubious conduct of a distant war but one cannot lie to the House of Commons!

Perhaps it was another aspect of the Falklands War which continued to cause concern. Several different sources, in Government, in the Ministry of Defence and even from within the Polaris fleet, have informed Tam Dalyell and others that a Polaris missile submarine *was* ordered on patrol in the South Atlantic within missile range of Argentina during the Falklands War. There were Soviet hunter-killer submarines also active in the South Atlantic and the Polaris submarine had to be protected by escorting hunter-killer submarines, even to the extent of depleting the numbers of these submarines available to guard the Task Force itself. Early in May 1982, at the height of the conflict, there were only two hunter-killer submarines available in the war zone to protect the entire Task Force, and only one of these was fully operational.

This information, while from diverse and invariably highly-placed sources, is verbal rather than documentary and as long as that remains the case is unlikely to become an issue of national controversy. Yet it must be a constant worry to Government that an unhappy mole will provide Tam Dalyell with firm evidence of this act—evidence quite capable of inflicting terminal damage on the Government as its appalling implications become clear.

The Peruvian peace proposals and the Polaris submarine are matters of long term concern. In the run up to Tam Dalyell's motion on 6 June, it may well have been the most recent banana skin, the Westland affair, which was the greatest worry, and central to that was the leaking of the Law Officer's letter. Tam Dalyell asserts that the leak was planned before the letter was even written. He further asserts that this information comes from senior officials of the Department of Trade and Industry present at a dinner for the visiting Turkish Minister of Technology shortly after the Westland affair reached its climax.

Some days before he was to deliver his speech, Tam Dalyell sought the help of the staff of the House of Commons Library in getting from the Department of Trade and Industry a guest list of those present at the dinner. This request apparently caused great concern in the Department of Trade and Industry. Shortly afterwards, the filibuster was organised and Tam Dalyell's debate in the House was lost.

*   *   *   *   *   *

Whatever the motives of those who prevented the Dalyell motion from being put on 6 June, the effect was to focus once more on the matter of integrity in Government. Some would argue that the Government's behaviour over the Libyan raid and the Westland affair show an almost indecent propensity for following US interests, perhaps originating in the debt owed to the United States over the Prime Minister's greatest achievement, the Falklands victory. Tam Dalyell is more concerned with behaviour towards the House of Commons and the electorate. He believes that all three episodes illustrate one thing: an arrogance borne of a contempt for the norms of Parliamentary Democracy.

Thus the Government lies consistently over the *Belgrano* incident, even to the extent of seeking deliberately to mis-

lead a Select Committee. The Prime Minister insists that
Britain had to be involved in the Libyan raid, even though
military authorities in the United States dispute this. Finally, a senior Minister who has become a dangerous embarrassment is damaged by the Government-inspired leaking
of a confidential letter from a Law Officer.

This is the essence of Tam Dalyell's case and it was this
case which Conservative Members of Parliament, with the
knowledge and approval of the Prime Minister, prevented
him from arguing on the floor of the House. It is ironic
that members of a Government purporting to be so strong
in its support for freedom of speech in universities and elsewhere should successfully prevent such freedom of speech
within the House itself.

At the time of writing we have up to two years to the
next general election. During that time Tam Dalyell will continue to dig deep, aided perhaps by an occasional mole. He
may well uncover more interesting details of the Westland
affair and the Libyan incident. He might well sort out the
matter of the Peruvian peace bid during the Falklands War.
He might, just, succeed in answering the most important
question of all—just what was a Polaris missile submarine
doing in the South Atlantic in May 1982?

20 June 1986   Paul Rogers

Thatcher: Patterns of Deceit

A Friday, Mr Speaker, in this House is traditionally, usually, and rightly, a day, not for Party business, but for the business of the House of Commons. Today's business is, as far as I'm concerned, no exception. In initiating this Debate on the Conduct of the Prime Minister, I do so, not as a party politician, which I unashamedly am, but, on this occasion, as a Child of the House of Commons, who, after twenty-four years in this place, has come to care very much about the way in which the House is treated, by Ministers, however exalted.

Above all, this Debate is about Candour—whether the right hon. Lady the Prime Minister has, on three crunch issues, been candid with the House, and not least with her own colleagues, Backbench and Ministerial.

Let us first of all address ourselves to a House of Commons point on the Falklands. Four hon. Friends of mine 'sweated their proverbial guts out, without the expert assistance of Clerks of the House that is available to a Select Committee Chairman, to produce a major and tightly-argued Minority Report on the events of 1st/2nd May 1982.

Any one of us, from whatever side of the House, who has come to know these four hon. Friends of mine, knows perfectly well, that they care deeply about the House of Commons, and the role of the Backbencher, and are sceptical men, of independent judgement. I would guess

that one of the basic reasons why the hon. Members for
Bow and Poplar [Ian Mikardo] , New Ham [Nigel Spearing] ,
Falkirk West [Dennis Canavan] and Doncaster [Michael
Welsh] went to such lengths in terms of time and effort
was that they perceived many unexplained inconsistencies
in the Government's account of 1st/2nd May 1982, and in
subsequent information that came to them from the Old
Bailey trial of Clive Ponting and elsewhere, such as Arthur
Gavshon and Desmond Rice's book on the sinking of the
Belgrano.

This motion gives further opportunity to my friends to
try to winkle the truth out of the Government. My hon.
Friends can speak for themselves, if they catch your eye;
for my part, I would like simply to confine myself to repeat-
ing their questions:

1. At what date and on what grounds did the War Cabinet
   abandon its prime purpose of deploying and using
   military action in support of diplomatic initiative and
   economic pressure for a negotiated settlement and
   change to a 'military solution' as the main criterion
   for action?
2. In addition to official communications, what information, if any, about the Peruvian peace initiative did
   the Prime Minister or other Ministers receive from
   other sources, including the United States Embassy in
   Lima, or sources in Britain or elsewhere?
3. What intercepts were made, and when, of orders to
   the Argentine fleet; which of them were decoded, and
   when; which of the decrypts were passed to Northwood,
   and when; and which were then passed to the War
   Cabinet, and when? Were the *Guardian* and *Observer*
   reports [5 January 1985 and 6 January 1985 respect-
   ively] on this matter correct?

*The House of Commons deserves an answer to these
questions.*

Mr Speaker, I do not believe in innuendo, and so let
me not mince my words. I believe that the Prime Minister
misled the House of Commons in a number of ways over
the Falklands War, but in particular over the timing of
when she had the 'first indications' of the Peruvian peace
proposals. After my meeting with the Prime Minister in
her room in the House at 9.30pm on Wednesday, 21
April 1982, I went back, alarmed, to tell my colleagues
that in the absence of the humiliation of Argentina, she
wanted a fight. This assessment is confirmed by Sarah
Keays in her book, *A Question of Judgement* (pp. 28-29):

> For all the public discussion of settlement proposals, it
> was clear from what Cecil [Parkinson] told me that the
> Inner Cabinet, like most of the population, privately
> believed that war was unavoidable. On Sunday, 18th
> April, Cecil came to see me very late and rather angry. It
> was the only time I heard him make serious criticism of
> the Prime Minister, for whom he had great admiration,
> being deeply impressed by her courage and determination.
> He was infuriated by an exchange he had had with her at
> a meeting of the Inner Cabinet with the Chiefs of Staff.
> When he had expressed his concern about the risks attend-
> ant on a particular course of action, one of several under
> consideration, she had rounded on him with words to
> the effect that there was no room for faint hearts in the
> Inner Cabinet.

I thought it a very telling incident. If the Prime Minister's
closest colleagues could not feel free to express their
opinions to her absolutely frankly, they could be of no use
to her at all.

Against this background, why was the House of Commons

being told repeatedly that we were doing everything possible to find a peaceful solution, and why was the Foreign Secretary, the right hon. Gentleman for Cambridgeshire [Francis Pym] sent off to Washington in what he imagined were bona fide peace initiatives?

Secondly, as I have argued several times, it is simply not true that as the Prime Minister said to the Shadow Cabinet, in her letter to my right hon. Friend for Llanelli [Denzil Davies] that 'the first indications of the Peruvian Peace Proposals reached London at 11.15 pm on Sunday, 2nd May'.

Before moving on from the Falklands, may I spatchcock into my speech a point that saddens me about Select Committees? On Wednesday, 16 January 1985, it appears from the record (page lix) that five hon. Conservative Members of the Select Committee voted against even putting questions to the Defence Secretary, Lord Lewin, Sir John Nott, the Foreign Secretary and the Prime Minister.

It would be hypocritical of me to be critical of these five Conservatives because I remember very well when, in 1966, as a Member of the Select Committee on Science and Technology, doing a major Report on the British Nuclear Power Programme, I suggested that the then Prime Minister, Harold Wilson, should come before the Committee to answer questions that I thought were appropriate to the Head of Government. Wrath descended on my unsuspecting head, from all quarters, including Fred Peart, the then Leader of the House, and the late Dick Crossman, whose PPS I was. It was made clear to me in colourful language, that it was above my station in life to suggest the hauling of the Prime Minister in front of the Select Committee. Although in retrospect I was justified and right to ask that Harold Wilson should testify on the subject of nuclear power—I caved in.

Therefore all I can say to Parliamentary colleagues of all Parties is that if we put our trust in Select Committees in

doing a proper investigative job on sensitive issues in cases
where the actions of a Prime Minister and Head of Government are concerned, we shall be disappointed. Since, as
Bagehot and others have pointed out, the House of Commons is not only a legislature, like the U.S. Congress, but
also a 'pool of talent' from which the Executive is selected,
considerations of decorum, possible preferment to Ministerial office and sheer honourable party loyalty make it
inevitable that Select Committees cannot by their nature be
expected to be satisfactory instruments of investigation
into Prime Ministerial conduct.

* * * * * *

Therefore I do not apologise for using time on the floor
of the House to consider Libya and the F1-11s, which is
currently being looked at by the Defence Select Committee,
and Westlands, which is being looked at by the Select Committees on Defence, Trade and Industry.

Mr Speaker, on 14 April, at 3.30pm, I rose on this point
of order concerning Libya:

Mr Speaker: Does it arise out of questions?
Mr Dalyell: Yes. Precisely because I did not put in a
    private notice question I feel that, on behalf of several
    Back Benchers, I am entitled to ask whether it is not
    extraordinary that, in the middle of the crisis concern-
    ing Libya and the British bases, the House of Commons
    is to hear nothing. Would not any visitor consider it
    extraordinary if we were to spend eight and a half
    hours debating Sunday trading and yet, as a Legislature,
    be told nothing about the United States or Soviet
    position or to have a statement on the crisis?
    You will know, Mr Speaker, that I have thought for
    a long time that you are a very superior Speaker to
    George Thomas. *[Interruption.]*

Mr Speaker: Order. I am enjoying this.

Mr Dalyell: George Thomas made certain judgments of
his own, such as that in April 1982 that the Prime
Minister ought to be supported on the south Atlantic
issue. We read that in his memoirs. There is no secret
about it. That happened during one of the last crises,
when he was Speaker, concerning those islands in the
south Atlantic. Do you think, Mr Speaker, that it is
matter of some judgment whether circumstances that
are a matter of war, or potential war, outside Europe,
entitle Parliament to a report from Ministers? There
might be a judgment about the safety of British subjects. You know that I am one of those hon. Members
who have constituents who are involved, and at risk,
near Tripoli. Bearing in mind the circumstances, why
does the House not have at least a Foreign Office or
Prime Ministerial report on this urgent matter?

Though I believe your motives were honourable, Mr Speaker,
it will be deemed a great pity that you did not grant a
Private Notice Question to Denis Healey, as the obvious
question would have been asked about the use of British
bases,* and the House of Commons would have had some
input into events before they took place, rather than a post
mortem. However, I suppose one can understand a Prime
Minister's decision not to reveal the use of British bases before
an attack. What the House of Commons deserves to know,
is to what extent her senior colleagues were consulted. For
example, the Secretary of State for Defence, George
Younger, said on radio, in answer to a question about the
'position of the Government were the Americans determin-
ed to use forces mustered in the UK in the Mediterranean—
F1-11 bombers based in Southern England':

*The obvious question was whether permission would have been
granted to the Americans for their use crucially in non-NATO circumstances, i.e. for an American operation?

The question is whether such a strike would be counted
as normal operations, or not, and all I can say is that we,
if we received such a request, we would look at it very
sympathetically, bearing in mind that our American allies,
and they are allies, spending a lot of money defending
ourselves, they are having their civilians, innocent civilians,
murdered, and we cannot just allow that to go on.
Interviewer: To what degree are British forces involved, I
am thinking particularly of the surveillance bases on
Cyprus?
Well, there is no British involvement and there has been
no suggestion of any British involved . . . of British forces,
of British weapons or British bases or anything like that.
There is of course normal intelligence covering system
which operates all the time of day, every day throughout
the year and that information is pooled between us and
the Americans to our great advantage, and that is made
available and so to that extent we have an involvement.

Younger's answer implies that he had no notion what his
Prime Minister had already agreed with President Reagan.
As his Scottish Parliamentary colleague for twenty-two
years, my judgement is that the right hon. Gentleman for
Ayr would not have said that, unless he believed it to be
true at the time he said it.

When was the Foreign Secretary, Sir Geoffrey Howe,
consulted? Was it *after*, or *before* anything could be usefully
done to act on the considered advice of the Foreign Office?
Replying in this House to the right hon. Gentleman for
Leeds' [Denis Healey] question as to whether he knew at
the Hague negotiations that the United States 'was about
to launch the taskforce, with British agreement and support,
a few hours later', Sir Geoffrey stated:

There was scarcely any mention of the United States

intention. No evidence emerged during the discussion
that any Foreign Minister was aware during the meeting
of a final American decision to attack. For my part, I
had no confirmation of any decision by the President,
still less of any decision to authorise raids that night, until
I came back to London and met the Prime Minister.

These questions are not simply Opposition mischief-making.
In his remarkable speech in the Other Place, 18 April (col-
umn 894), Field-Marshal Lord Carver recalled that the Prime
Minister said that discussions with the President covered a
week. The Field-Marshal asked Lady Young to tell the House
who was consulted and who agreed. To date the Field-
Marshal's questions have gone unanswered. The House of
Commons deserves an answer.

The House of Commons is also entitled to press the Prime
Minister as to her real motives for agreeing to the use of
British bases. The following exchange took place here
between Jonathan Aitken, John McWilliam and the Prime
Minister on 15 April 1986:

Mr Aitken: When my right hon. Friend took the difficult
but wholly correct decision to permit the use of British
bases for the United States attack, was she influenced
not only by loyalty to an ally with a just cause, but by
a much more practical consideration: that fewer risks
were likely to be caused to Libyan civilians and to
United States military personnel if the United States
used the much more precise equipment, the F1-11,
rather than carrier-based aircraft?

The Prime Minister: Yes, Sir. My hon. Friend is correct.
That was a factor in the decision to use our bases and
why those aircraft were especially right for the action
that was undertaken. We were also influenced by the
fact that the United States has hundreds of thousands

of forces in Europe to defend the liberty of Europe. In that capacity they have been subject to terrorist attack. It was inconceivable to me that we should refuse United States aircraft and pilots the opportunity to defend their people.

Mr McWilliam: Why did the Prime Minister choose to authorise the use of British bases for this attack when the capability to mount that attack existed with the battle fleet not 300 miles north of the coast of Libya?

The Prime Minister: As my hon. Friend the Member for Thanet, South (Mr Aitken) indicated in an earlier question, the F1-11s were required because they are more accurate on particular targets and because they would involve far less collateral damage and far less risk to American pilots. The Americans are our allies and put considerable effort into defending the freedom of Europe. I hope that the hon. Gentleman on the Opposition Benches will remember that.

In general, the impression was given that the Prime Minister gave permission because she was above all concerned to limit civilian casualties.

Yet, from the Pentagon come very different reasons. Firstly, the attack on Libya provided a proving ground for weapons. *US News and World Report* carries an article by William Broyles, Junior, 12 May 1986, on 'The Politics of War', in which he writes:

The budget, in short, is the mission. 'It all comes back to the budget,' says one ex-Pentagon analyst.

For years we've been saying that radar, infra-red, and smart bombs are the way to go. We've spent billions on night-mission avionics, so we had to try to use them, even if a daylight strike would have been better.

Equally bluntly, *Aviation Week* of 21 April asserted that
the attack on Libya 'provided a good proving ground for
the F1-11s to be flown in the Mediterranean, and gave the
Air Force a chance to demonstrate its capabilities'. A raid
of this kind was deemed to have great value in the presentation to Congress of the case for greater spending on the
US Navy and US Air Force. However, it was not a reason
given by our Prime Minister to our House of Commons.

Secondly, there was inter-service rivalry involved between
the US Navy and the US Air Force. As a senior official of
the Pentagon artlessly put it to *Aviation Week* (21 April,
page 19): 'Understandably, after the all-Navy action in
Libya last month, the Air Force wanted a piece of the
action'. Again, this was not a reason given by our Prime
Minister to our House of Commons, for the use of our
territory in Britain, as a base for non-Nato operations.

Thirdly, there has been the formidable lobby in the
Pentagon which has been championing the idea of joint
service operations, particularly the use of land-based aircraft
in support of naval operations. When the Joint Chiefs of
Staff sat down in December 1985 to consider the military
options against Libya, the Chief of Naval Operations,
Admiral James Watkins, and others, saw a useful opportunity for a joint Naval-Air Force operation to demonstrate
the value of their concept to doubters in Congress and the
Pentagon. Again, this was not a reason hinted at by our
Prime Minister to our House of Commons.

It is simply not true that the bomb-aiming equipment on
the F1-11s was superior to the bomb-aiming equipment on
the carrier-borne A-7s. They both had the TRAM system,
or its equivalent.

Fourthly, and possibly most important of all from the
point of view of the House of Commons, whereas certainly
the internal politics of the US military were an important
reason for the attacks on Libya, the nature and timing of

the raid had much wider political implications. I quote from the April 1986 issue of *Sanity* where, on page 18, Dan Pleasch asks Rear-Admiral Eugene Carroll Junior, of the Center for Defence Information in Washington: 'In your experience, would it have been practical to use the F1-11s, and ask the British afterwards?' 'That was the basis,' said Carroll, 'on which the plan was prepared'.

Mr Speaker, the implications are chilling. A major reason for including the F1-11s in the operation was to tie in Britain, as one European country seen to be supporting the United States.

Again, this was not a reason the Prime Minister offered to the House of Commons.

On 3 June, I asked the Prime Minister in a specific oral question if she would:

> ... list those characteristics of the F1-11 aircraft based in the United Kingdom which rendered their use essential for the United States' attack on Libya.
> The Prime Minister: The F1-11 aircraft based in the United Kingdom provided the best equipped means of carrying out the United States operation against specific terrorist targets in Libya, with the lowest possible risk of Libyan civilian and United States service casualties. As the United States has indicated, the F1-11 possesses advanced avionics and other capabilities which made it particularly suitable for such a mission.
> Mr Dalyell: Will the Prime Minister name the senior American, or Americans, who told her that the F1-11s were more precise than the carrier-based aircraft?
> The Prime Minister: That was the advice that we received both from across the Atlantic and from home.
> Sir Anthony Buck [Chairman of the Conservative Defence committee] : Does my right hon. Friend agree that if

we had not given permission for the F1-11s to be util-
ised, the Americans would have gone ahead, used less
accurate aircraft and that there would have been more
civilian casualties?

The Prime Minister: As I said when I spoke to the House
on this matter, I understand that the raid would have
gone ahead in any event.

When pressed, the Prime Minister becomes uncharacter-
istically vague about the question of what she was told by
the Americans. In *The Scotsman*, Martin Dowle asserts that
President Reagan did not talk personally to the Prime Minister in the week before the Libyan raid. What senior
American, then, speaking to our Prime Minister implied
that the expensive carrier-borne A-6s and A-7s were so
inferior to the F1-11s, that they could not carry out the
Libya mission? Any American who said that would have
some awkward questions from the US Navy and US tax-
payers back in Washington. I call upon the Prime Minister
to let us know who exactly did tell her, if he did, about
the F1-11s being more precise, avoiding collateral damage
and cutting down civilian casualties? The Prime Minister
has got to the stage where she will invent any cock and
bull story that suits her.

The Minister replying to the debate may switch ground
and claim, as the Prime Minister did in answer to the hon.
Member for Thanet, South [Jonathan Aitken] on 15 April
1986 (*Hansard*, col. 726): 'We were also influenced by the
fact that the United States has hundreds of thousands of
forces in Europe to defend the liberty of Europe. In that
capacity they have been subject to terrorist attack.' If this
is a reference to the bombing in West Berlin, could the
House of Commons be told why the Federal Police in West
Germany, the Bundeskriminalamt, have even now refused
to confirm the Libyan connection? Why Herr Lochte, the

Chief of the Verfassungschutz, the Bureau for the Protection of the Constitution, has gone on record to say that he excludes any Libyan connection? And why the German Intelligence, the Bundesnachrichtendienst, differs substantially from the Americans about the interpretation of Libyan messages?

I am no admirer of Mr Botha, but Mr Botha was quite justified in making comparisons between what our Prime Minister and President Reagan did and the attack, so universally deplored, on Zimbabwe, Zambia and Botswana.

I should point out, Mr Speaker, that it's not just the Prime Minister's critics who think along these lines. Ferdinand Mount in *The Spectator* of 24 May 1986 (page 6) writes:

> For the comparison does throw a fascinating if rather eerie light on our confused and contradictory attitudes towards terrorism and the response to terrorism. The two raids are as nearly alike as any two events in an untidy world. The Governments of Zambia, Botswana and Zimbabwe may not sponsor terrorism in quite the same way as Colonel Gaddafi does; but the distinction is not a crucial one.

*   *   *   *   *   *

I should now like to turn to the third 'crunch' issue. Mr Speaker, my Parliamentary interest in Westlands began long before the company's name became a household word. Urged to take an interest in the British helicopter industry by Mr Clive Jenkins, Mr Stan Davidson and Mr Robert McCusker, at our monthly working meetings of ASTMS* MPs, back in June-July 1985, I went on delegations to Ministers about Westland's orders and visited the Yeovil plant on 18 November. My interest in subsequent events was rendered sceptical by the fact that, in November 1985,
*Association of Supervisory, Technical and Managerial Staff.

as the hon. Member for Yeovil [Paddy Ashdown] knows,
they could hardly get a Minister, including Ministers at
Defence, to take any interest at all in their plight.

Mr Speaker, by comparison with the Falklands War and
the F1-11 attack on Libya, the Westland Affair may seem
from the point of view of history, somewhat insignificant.
Yet it obsessed the country for three weeks and understandably so, since it illuminated the heart of government.

Mr Speaker, in this House, we all have to make judgements
about one another, often over a longish period of time. I
simply say that, having experience of the right hon. Gentleman, the Member for Richmond [Leon Brittan] over some
forty-five Parliamentary days when he was the Opposition
Spokesman on Devolution and having seen him in action
since—I find it hard to believe that he, a QC, a careful
lawyer, a former Home Secretary, would have been so reckless as himself to dream up the idea of leaking selectively a
Law Officer's letter to a Minister of the Crown. Yet, if such
a ploy would not occur to *him*, it might well occur to *her*—
for the Prime Minister has a reckless streak and, had she
not been a gambler, she would never have taken on the
right hon. Gentleman for Bexley [Edward Heath] and
become Leader of her Party.

However, it is more than Parliamentary instinct which
suggests—to borrow the image used by the right hon.
Gentleman the Member for Devonport [David Owen]—
that the strands of the spider's web of the Mayhew letter
led to Downing Street. One should not repeat gossip, but
Alan Watkins puts in print in *The Observer* that senior Conservatives have said to him, 'Poor Leon carries the can!'—
and I must say this seems to be accepted as the received
wisdom of Westminster. Are we then simply to shrug our
shoulders? 'Carrying the can' for whom? Only for one
person—she who told my hon. Friend the Member for
Bolsover [Dennis Skinner] 'I did not know about the then

Secretary of State for Trade and Industry's own role in the matter of the disclosure until the enquiry had reported'. Now, however, the House of Commons finds itself far beyond circumstantial gossip. For a major newspaper has published a book, *Not with Honour*, written by two award-winning journalists, Magnus Linklater and David Leigh, which has to be answered—and this House is the place to do it. Let me say at once that there are certain minor inaccuracies in the book, for example the Chairman of the 1922 Committee has been awarded a premature knighthood by the authors: he is Mr and not Sir Cranley Onslow, but many substantial questions remain.

Consider, first of all, the terms of this letter from the Prime Minister to her Trade Secretary:

My dear Leon,

I am very sorry that despite all the arguments I could use I was unable to dissuade you this afternoon from resigning . . .
It was my wish that you should remain as a Member of the Cabinet . . .
I hope that it will not be long before you return to high office to continue your Ministerial career.

Uniquely, as far as I know, the Prime Minister hopes for his return to 'high office'. How could she say this if the full story was of a trusted Cabinet Minister who had deceived her, by withholding the truth, for over a fortnight?

On page 167 of the same book the authors report one Tory backbencher as saying: 'What I minded most of all was the aura of seedy incompetence it exposed'. Mr Speaker, I do not know who said this to the authors, but I'll vouch that a Conservative Member of Parliament, for whom I have considerable respect, used exactly the same phraseology in my hearing.

'Seedy incompetence' is a serious enough charge against
one's own Prime Minister, but as Linklater and Leigh put it,
again on page 167, another senior Tory was even more out-
spoken: 'It was a pack of lies,' he said. Mr Speaker, I don't
wish to sound pompous, priggish, or even politically partisan
but I was not sent here by the electors of the Linlithgow
constituency to accept packs of lies from Prime Ministers.

Another serious charge raised by Linklater and Leigh is
that on the morning of the right hon. Gentleman for Richmond's [Leon Brittan] resignation, his 'friend and mentor
Geoffrey Howe called to urge him to stay'. Mr Speaker, I
understand that the authors are accurate in this assertion.
But is the House of Commons really to believe that our
Foreign Secretary made such a call on a Minister, however
close, whatever the political protegé relationship, if he
thought that the whole story was that of the Trade Secretary
withholding information from his closest colleagues for over
a fortnight and deceiving the Prime Minister? For the Foreign
Secretary to have behaved in this way, it is necessary to
assume that the right hon. Gentleman for Reigate [Geoffrey
Howe], whatever else he thought, did not think that the
right hon. Gentleman for Richmond deserved to take the
blame. *The House of Commons is entitled to an explanation
from the Foreign Secretary as to exactly why, in the circumstances, he took the trouble to take an initiative and urge
the right hon. Gentleman for Richmond to remain in office.*

Another point raised by the authors of *Not with Honour*,
on page 168, is that 'Brittan telephoned Whitelaw who said
the same'—that is, that he should remain in office. Now,
Mr Speaker, twenty-four years ago, Willie Whitelaw MP,
Junior Minister and Under-Secretary at the old Ministry of
Labour, used to answer my questions on unemployment
in the West Lothian constituency. When one went on
delegation, he was helpful and courteous. I have known him

ever since, particularly when I was the late Richard Crossman's PPS, and Willie Whitelaw, as he then was, was the Opposition Chief Whip. Granted that he is a patron of the right hon. Gentleman for Richmond and helped to get him his North of England seat, I do not believe that it is in the character of Willie Whitelaw to urge a Minister to remain in office if, in the noble lord's opinion, that Minister had behaved badly—let alone concealed the truth from his colleagues for a fortnight. Lord Whitelaw, by his action in asking the Trade Secretary to stay, must know that the blame lies elsewhere—and elsewhere can only be Number 10 Downing Street. Frankly, unlike the case of the Foreign Secretary's call, where I have corroborative information, I do not have corroborative evidence of the call to Lord Whitelaw. However, if such a call did not take place, Lord Whitelaw should take immediate steps to repudiate it and a retraction from the authors. If such a call did take place, then *the House of Commons deserves to know from Lord Whitelaw, who was our trusted colleague for a quarter of a century, how he explains his call to a Minister, who has supposedly behaved so badly, to remain in office.*

There is, then, the role of Sir Gordon Reece. My hon. Friend the Member for Warrington [Douglas Hoyle], ex-President of ASTMS, whom whom I have a high regard, is for ever telling me that we ought to know more about the role of Sir Gordon. I refer again to *Not with Honour*, where (pages 60-62) the authors reveal that Sir Gordon Reece is hired as Consultant to Westlands unknown to the right hon. Gentleman for Henley [Michael Heseltine] and that he is regularly invited to spend Christmas Day with the Prime Minister and her family. On page 83 they assert that 'from now on' [Christmas 1985] 'his intimate knowledge of the workings of Downing Street and his close friendship with the Prime Minister would be even greater assets in helping to steer Westland through the political manoeuvrings that lay ahead.' *The Prime Minister who was keen enough to send Clive Ponting to the Old Bailey, should tell us about Sir Gordon's role, and whether he signed the Official Secrets Act, and if so, when?*

On 27 January 1986, the Political Editor of *The Financial Times*, Mr Peter Riddell, wrote in his newspaper:

> The story then enters murkier territory. Given Mr Brittan's admission that he consulted Sir Patrick [Mayhew] that weekend, who suggested the writing of a letter to Mr Heseltine? The Westland Affair also appears to have been discussed by the Prime Minister and advisers at Chequers that Sunday.
>
> A big question about the existing official version is raised by the fact that Sir John Cuckney knew possibly on Saturday and definitely on Sunday, 24 hours before Sir Patrick's letter was sent—that the Solicitor General had reservations about Mr Heseltine's letter of the previous Friday. Indeed, the Westland Camp was seeking, on the Sunday afternoon, to make this point known so as to discredit Mr Heseltine.
>
> This raises the key issue of how Sir John learnt of Sir Patrick's doubts. Was he told of them by Mr Brittan or by the Downing Street staff?

I believe that Sir Gordon Reece was the link man with Sir John Cuckney, and tipped him off. Can the Prime Minister deny it?

Linklater and Leigh again claim, on page 168 of their book, that at a meeting at the Department of Trade and Industry, Sir Brian Hayes, the Permanent Secretary, and the other senior officials were against him going. 'They argued that, despite the heat engendered in the House, nothing fundamental had changed. . . . The politicians were less certain. They had talked to Tory MPs and knew what

their mood was. They thought the prospects for survival
were bleak.' Of course Sir Brian Hayes did not think that
his Secretary of State should resign—because he knew very
well from the Chief Press Officer in the Department,
Colette Bowe, and others at the DTI who was the major
instigator of the offence of the selective leak. People who
know Sir Brian Hayes tell me that they find it inconceivable that this upright and impressive Civil Servant should
have urged a Minister to stay if he thought he was guilty of
prolonged deceit of the Prime Minister. How discreet Sir
Brian Hayes is, I do not know, but I take it on my responsibility to say that it seems to be common talk in the
Athenaeum and the Reform Club, and in the upper echelons
of Whitehall, that Sir Brian still considers the right hon.
Gentleman for Richmond ill done by.
Does the Prime Minister challenge the Linklater/Leigh
account of this meeting at the Department of Trade and
Industry? And, if not, how does she explain the unanimous
view of the Civil Servants present? The Civil Servants had
no axe to grind. The politicians who wanted the right hon.
Gentleman for Richmond to leave office, and demurred at
the meeting, may have had their own political calculations.
*The House of Commons deserves to know what Sir Brian
Hayes and his senior colleagues know about the state of
knowledge of the Prime Minister.*
  Nor is it acceptable to place the onus on Mrs Thatcher's
Private Secretary, Mr Charles Powell, and her Press
Secretary, Mr Bernard Ingham. If Mr Powell really behaved
so badly, why has he remained in his job? Why hasn't he
been eased out? The only reason can be that he was indeed
carrying out the Prime Minister's wishes. From the Adjourn-
ment Debate on 28 April 1986 the House will accept that I
am hardly Mr Bernard Ingham's most uncritical admirer,
but fair's fair and, whatever he did or didn't do, the right
hon. Lady has responsibility for his actions. Members on

all sides find it simply incredible that these two people, Mr
Ingham and the Prime Minister, should see so much of
each other during their working lives, and that it never
occurred to the Prime Minister to ask Mr Ingham what he
knew of the issue that was endangering her Government.
Linklater and Leigh make the same point:

> The sequence of events as recounted by the Prime Min-
> ister was, indeed, incredible, for it required MPs to
> believe that she had never herself asked a single pertinent
> question about a scandalous action which directly affect-
> ed her government. . . . To accept Mrs Thatcher's full
> explanation it was necessary to believe that both she and
> Bernard Ingham had behaved entirely out of character;
> that she had never thought to ask a man in her own
> office, and with whom she worked in conditions of great
> intimacy, how a leak of major political significance had
> been effected; and that he, who knew more about the
> art of leaking than any other man in the country, had
> never told her what had happened. It showed a Prime
> Minister, apparently unable to control her own officials,
> but approving of the use of smear tactics against a fellow
> Minister.*

However, out of the window goes any old-fashioned
doctrine of *ministerial responsibility* nowadays. Shades of
Sir Thomas Dugdale and Crichel Down, which must be
ancient history! The notion that Ministers ought actually
go as far as resigning, because of failures of their Civil
Servants may belong to a bygone age. In its place we now
appear to have a very different doctrine indeed. The doctrine
that is now before us is that if a senior Minister or a Prime
Minister find themselves in a jam of their own making, they

*Not with Honour by Magnus Linklater and David Leigh, with Ian
Mather, is published by Sphere Books.

can blame the Civil Servants. (The Prime Minister's image
is one of courage, but blaming Civil Servants for one's own
actions is not courage, but cowardice.) This novel doctrine
in Britain should be unacceptable to any self-respecting,
honourable House of Commons.

But, of course, all these things and more can be explained
by the fact—I repeat *fact*—that the right hon. Lady for Finchley
did indeed know about the leak from a very early stage. On
pages 142-3 of their book, Linklater and Leigh write:

Sir Michael Havers, who had just returned to his duties,
had found his deputy, Patrick Mayhew, in a state of rage.
As Havers wrote, the unauthorised leak of a classified
letter from one Minister to another was a serious matter.
He therefore suggested that Armstrong should set up one
of the 'leak inquiries' which were such a regular feature
of the Thatcher administration, and had so publicly in
the past led to the arrest of civil servants under the
Official Secrets Act.

Curiously, Mrs Thatcher did not seem to spring on
this suggestion with her usual zeal, although she discussed it with her staff. 'I was told that the Solicitor-General's
advice had not been disclosed by *my* office,' she says. 'I
did not know about Leon Brittan's own role.'

Mrs Thatcher may indeed not have known precisely
how Leon Brittan's departmental discussions had been
arranged. Nor, as her subsequent behaviour made quite
clear, did she particularly care. She did not institute an
inquiry.

Instead, following Havers's complaint, she spoke priv-
ately to Brittan about the leak. Although this is something
the Prime Minister has failed to disclose, to widespread
disbelief, the evidence comes from an authoritative source,
who told us: 'The Prime Minister knew about the leak.
She was pleased it had been done. There was a meeting

between Brittan and her after the complaint from Mayhew. Only the two of them were present . . . Brittan assumed she knew of [the leak's] origins. You must draw your own conclusions.'

One of Brittan's friends adds, 'Nobody thought it was a problem. The complaints were out of the public domain and any inquiry was expected to be a formality. Leon wasn't worried at all about it.'*

I do not know precisely when this meeting between the Prime Minister and Leon Brittan took place. I do know the authoritative source from which it was revealed. The source was in a position to know, at the centre of Government. I challenge the Prime Minister, if she disputes the source, even if she understandably does not like litigation, at least to ask for a retraction. Her failure to do so can only be interpreted as acquiescence that Linklater and Leigh and their source are indeed accurate.

The House of Commons deserves to know what the Prime Minister is going to do about Linklater and Leigh, pages 142-3.

It cannot, yet again, just be left in limbo.

I, Mr Speaker, will go further than Linklater and Leigh, and I will repeat it outside the Chamber so as not to shelter under the cloak of privilege. I say that the Solicitor-General was lured by the Prime Minister, with the reluctant con- nivance of the Trade Secretary into writing a letter which the Prime Minister intended to be leaked, selectively or otherwise, from before the very moment it was suggested to the Law Officer. In other words, the Solicitor-General was set-up by the Prime Minister into writing a letter, when he genuinely had no notion of the purpose for which it was intended, from the moment it was conceived in 10 Down-

Not with Honour by Magnus Linklater and David Leigh, with Ian Mather, is published by Sphere Books.

ing Street. The Solicitor-General, an honourable Law Officer, was had for a sucker, used and abused in a shameful way. No wonder the Solicitor-General contemplated resignation. It might be easy for me to suggest that he should have resigned, but it would have been an awesome responsibility: to have brought his whole Government tumbling down, for that might have been the effect, had he done so. Equally, the reason the Attorney-General was beside himself with rage on returning from his sick bed, was that he realised that his colleague, the Solicitor-General, had been set up. And yet, I have to say to the Law Officers of the Crown, what they undoubtedly know deep in their hearts. It is they who bear higher responsibilities than those of most honourable Members; they are symbols of our national respect for law, for justice, for morality in public life. When factors of political expediency transcend those centuries-old standards—it should come as no surprise to all of us here if the law, if justice as we practice it, if public morality fall into general disrepute. If we, as representatives of the people, are seen to be cutting corners, covering up the truth, flouting the traditions achieved and cherished by our forebears, we can have no right to complain if our fellow-citizens beyond the precincts of this Palace of Westminster begin to do the same. Deep issues are involved here.

It is not only the circumstantial evidence that makes me suspicious. I do not believe that a Solicitor-General reading *The Times* at home one Saturday morning says to himself, 'I must pen a hypersensitive letter to the Defence Secretary, complaining about his actions, as soon as I get back to the office'. If the House doubts my word, let a Select Committee, examine, under oath, members of the then private office of the right hon. Gentleman for Weybridge [Geoffrey Pattie].

Mr Speaker, for most of the extraordinary things about the leaked letter which MPs and the country have been

expected to believe, I do offer an explanation, to the House.
But, first, let me offer a preface. Often people say, 'What's
the point of Parliamentary Questions? What's the point of
debates and speeches in the House?' One thing about
Parliamentary activity is that those who focus on particular
subjects become the receptacles for information, which
would not otherwise come to us. After some press coverage in *The Times* Diary and *The Guardian* of this debate, I
was given the following information which I am authorised
to use, by a participant at a dinner for the Turkish Minister
of Technology, Mustafa Tinaz Titiz, on 30 January at
Lancaster House.

At this dinner officials of the Department of Trade and
Industry, in a position to know, raged about the behaviour
of politicians for all who cared to listen. They were
extremely angry at the fact that the blame for the leaking,
the selective leaking, of the Solicitor-General's letter had
been put on them and their colleagues at the DTI. It could
be argued, they said, that what the Prime Minister had told
the House of Commons, in a narrow sense, was technically
correct: that there were no telephone calls for 'permission
to leak or selectively leak'.

Why?

Because there was no need for such telephone calls.

*The agreement to leak had been reached between the
Prime Minister and an uneasy right hon. Gentleman for
Richmond, who had demurred, but was eager to please the
PM,* before *ever inducing the Solicitor-General to write a
letter to the then Defence Secretary* [Michael Heseltine].

When my right hon. Friend, the Leader of the Opposition
[Neil Kinnock], questioned the Prime Minister on her
actions, he did not get very far. Nor did I do any better,
nor any of the rest of us, because we were all like an audience
looking at a conjuror and looking at the wrong part of the
trick to see how the conjuror did it. The hanky panky of

the selective leaking was at the very beginning of the per-
formance and did not take place *after* the letter was
formulated. The latter was the point we were all looking
at, because even the most hardened of us had not expected
that degree of cynical, underhand behaviour from a British
Prime Minister.

To be fair to Colette Bowe, although she had the
instruction to leak from Mr Bernard Ingham, she certainly
kicked out against what she was being expected to do. The
House will remember that she said very little, but what she
did say in public was that every enquiry should be referred
to Number 10 Downing Street. No wonder! Nor, technically,
was Mr Bernard Ingham lying to the Armstrong Enquiry:
just possibly he did not discuss the leak *after* the letter had
been leaked, with the Prime Minister. Such a discussion
would have been superfluous, since Mr Ingham knew, *a
priori*, explicitly what the Prime Minister wanted done, and
what had been cooked up *beforehand* between the Prime
Minister and her uncomfortable Trade Secretary.

*Will the Minister answer the specific charge against his
Prime Minister that the 'dirty work', the decision to leak a
Law Officer's letter, took place before it was suggested to
the Solicitor-General that he should write the letter.*

Now, Mr Speaker, I hope that the Law Officers will study
what I have just said, because the House of Commons is
entitled to know what the right hon. Gentleman for Wimble-
don [Michael Havers] and the right hon. Gentleman for
Royal Tunbridge Wells [Patrick Mayhew] think about
what I have just said. Put in colloquial language, the
Solicitor-General was set-up, used and abused. No wonder
the Law Officers were reported as being on the very verge
of resignation. But I chide them not, because had they
resigned on this issue, at that time, their whole Government would have been at risk and that would be a fearful
responsibility to take on their shoulders.

However, the Law Officers do now owe the House of Commons the truth as to what did occur.

Let us be clear. It is nauseating what this Prime Minister has done in her tantrums. Mad with anger against her erstwhile Defence Secretary [Michael Heseltine], she and Bernard Ingham, with the eventual acquiescence, but against the better judgement of, her Trade Secretary [Leon Brittan], hit on the idea of putting the right hon. Gentleman for Henley wrong in law and making him look publicly foolish. So these three cook up the scheme of getting one of the Law Officers—the other one, the Attorney-General, was away sick—to send a letter, which they intended to leak wholly or in part. Leaking it, Mr Speaker, selectively or in full, was the *raison d'être* of the letter—that was its purpose —to do down the infernal nuisance, that the right hon. Gentleman for Henley had by then become. So they prompt the Solicitor-General to write his letter. The right hon. Gentleman for Tonbridge Wells [Sir Patrick Mayhew] imagines, naturally enough, that every Law Officer's letter to a Minister of the Crown is strictly confidential. In all innocence, he writes the letter. Routinely, a copy goes to Downing Street. I understand from those who have worked in Number 10, both under Lord Wilson and under the right hon. Gentleman for Bexley [Edward Heath] that any Law Officer's letter, because it may have consequences for the Courts, is handled with the utmost care, and rightly so.

Can one imagine the career diplomat, Mr Heath's Press Secretary, Sir Donald Maitland, using a Law Officer's letter for such a purpose. It is inconceivable! Moreover, it is a pertinent question to ask why a Law Officer's letter went anywhere near Mr Ingham's desk, unless the whole purpose was to make use, or abuse, of it in public? The only way in which the Downing Street Civil Service machine would allow a Law Officer's letter anywhere near the Press Office would be because they knew they had to act under Prime

Ministerial instruction.

To continue the narrative: Mr Bernard Ingham, knowing his Prime Minister's predetermined plan, orders a protesting Colette Bowe to leak the Solicitor-General's letter to Chris Moncrieff at the Press Association. They imagine that the leaked letter will serve its purpose of helping to discredit the right hon. Gentleman for Henley: that it will be a two-day wonder, ephemeral and quickly forgotten like so many two-day wonders in British politics. They take the view that the situation will be manageable, and that the House of Commons will, as usual, move on to other interests.

Unfortunately for the Prime Minister, an outraged Government employee, livid at the treatment of the Civil Service meted out to them by the Prime Minister, confirmed my information that it was Colette Bowe who phoned Mr Moncrieff, and that Miss Bowe acted under Ministerial and Prime Ministerial instructions. Otherwise, I would not have named her in this House. With the naming of Colette Bowe, the situation which the Prime Minister and her accomplices thought was manageable, became unmanageable. The paramount consideration now became the need to protect the position of the Prime Minister. The only way to do this was to put the onus, the blame, on understandings, or misunderstandings, between Civil Servants, no matter that it involved impugning, without good reason, the competence and integrity of Civil Servants caught up in an impossible situation.

Does not the House of Commons think that this is unacceptably immoral behaviour by major politicians?

Might I ask the Deputy Prime Minister [Lord Whitelaw], who may well have passed sleepless nights pondering what his duty was—what they would have made of regimental officers blaming their subordinates in this way for their own misdemeanours, in the mess of the Scots Guards? I say to Lord Whitelaw that the comparison with what his

Prime Minister has done is valid. *What questions is Lord Whitelaw going to ask?*

The Conservative knights of the shires, who populated the Government backbenches when I first arrived here, would turn in their graves if they knew that a character who behaved in this way towards Civil Servants, fellow humans, was leading their Party. By any standards, blaming the Civil Service for politicians' chicanery is unacceptable behaviour.

More culpable still is that, knowing full well her own role, the Prime Minister allowed, albeit unenthusiastically, an enquiry to go ahead. Authorising an enquiry, when a Prime Minister knows full well that she was responsible for the leak, that she instigated the very offence under investigation—is the action of a contemptible human being. If any of the rest of us were caught wasting police time, we should soon be in the dock. Is there one set of rules for a Prime Minister and another for the rest of the British people? The Prime Minister seems to believe there is!

I say to hon. Members opposite, and particularly those like the Home Secretary, with his particular responsibilities, that before he decides to go into the Government lobby at 2.30, he had better, to protect his great office, if nothing else, ascertain from Department of Trade and Industry officials precisely what happened and then confront his Prime Minister with her part in the affair.

Moreover, I ask the Government whips to let the Law Officers know what has been said—I rang their office to let them know I would refer to them—because the Attorney and the Solicitor-General had better be very clear about what really happened before they vote. Conservative Members of Parliament must ask themselves whether it is acceptable to them to be led by a person who allows, albeit reluctantly an enquiry to go ahead, when she knows that the leak which they are asked to investigate has been

propagated by herself, in connivance with her closest
inside associates, such as Ingham and Reece, and with the
reluctant connivance of the Secretary for Trade and Industry.

What the House of Commons has now to decide in the
light of Ministerial replies, is whether or not it deems that
the Prime Minister by her actions has brought the public
life of Britain into disrepute. Mr Speaker, it is for my
fellow Members of all parties to judge. In conclusion and as
proof that my concern is not simply a personal bee in the
bonnet, I reproduce the letter written by my right hon.
Friend, the Shadow Attorney General [John Morris QC
and Member for Aberavon] to the Prime Minister, together
with the right hon. Lady's exiguous response. As a former
Minister of State for Defence John Morris expresses his
careful and deep concern stemming from the Prime Minister's words.

HOUSE OF COMMONS
LONDON SWIA OAA

4th March 1986

Dear Prime Minister,

　　　　　　Thank you for your letter of the 24th
February, replying to my own of the 11th February. You

state in your letter that you have nothing to add to the 'full account' given in your statement to the House on the 23rd January and in the debate on the 27th January. Consequently, in search of the answers to the two questions which I have raised, I have re-read the parliamentary reports of both your statement and of the debate.

My first question was, 'Did you canvass with your advisers or any Minister before you requested, through your office, the Solicitor-General to write his letter, the possibility of the letter being put into the public domain?'

Nowhere in either of the reports which you cite can I find that you expressly said that you did, or that you did not, so canvass. Perhaps you might be so kind as to draw my attention to any passage on which you rely in this regard. In the absence of any express statement I have been obliged to consider what is implied by your statement and by your speech. An inference can be drawn that you did canvass the publication of the letter with someone. I say so for the following reasons:

1. You stress many times in your statement and in your speech that it was 'essential' (23 Jan. c. 458), 'vital' (23 Jan. c. 455) and 'of the first importance' (27 Jan. c. 651) to get into the public domain the knowledge that there were possible inaccuracies in the then Defence Secretary's letter of the 3rd January upon which judgments might be founded. Indeed, you go so far as to say that, 'it was a matter of duty that it should be made known publicly that there were thought to be material inaccuracies which ought to be corrected.' (23 Jan. c. 449).

2. It was 'in view of the continuing need for accuracy and consistency in government statements on this subject' (27 Jan. c. 632) that you asked that a message be sent to the Secretary of State for Trade and Industry, suggesting that he seek the Solicitor-

General's opinion. Considering the importance
which you attached to the accuracy of government
statements, and having regard to your view of your
duty, it would follow that, in seeking the Solicitor-
General's opinion, you intended it to be made
public in some way if it transpired that there were
inaccuracies or inconsistencies which needed correct-
ing.

3. On Saturday, 4th January, the Solicitor-General's
provisional view, that there were material inaccuracies which needed to be corrected, 'was reported' to
you (27 Jan. c. 652). You go on to say, 'The matter
could clearly not be left there.' (27 Jan. c. 652). I
take it from this that, conscious of your duty to
ensure and aware of the importance of ensuring the
accuracy and consistency of government statements,
you intended to make public your knowledge of
the possible inaccuracies. You say, 'I think that it
is essential to get into the public domain the fact
that there were possible inaccuracies which were
relevant to the situation.' (23 Jan. c. 458).

4. It appears, however, that once the Solicitor—General's provisional opinion was reported to you on
Saturday 4th January you took no obvious steps to
bring the matter to the public's attention notwith-
standing the fact that it was, as you say, 'urgent
that it should become public knowledge before
4pm that afternoon, 6 January.' (23 Jan. c. 450).
Instead, you say, 'I therefore, through my office,
asked him to consider writing to the Defence Secretary to draw that opinion to his attention.' (27 Jan.
c. 652).

5. In that such a letter would not, prima facie, put that
information into the public domain and in that you
attach great significance to that information being

put into the public domain and further in that, despite the urgency of the situation, you took no other steps towards putting that information into the public domain I am driven to conclude that you intended that the Solicitor-General's letter should be published in some way.

6. Further, you will recall that you said, 'It was to get that accurate information to the public domain that I gave my consent.' (23 Jan. c. 455). When questioned on this later you replied, 'I did not give my consent to the disclosure. It was not sought . . .' (27 Jan. c. 656). You will appreciate that this denial, which relates to the specific disclosure, does not negative the assertion that you consented to disclosure of the letter, as you originally stated.

7. Your office appear to have considered that to be the case. You say, 'They did not seek my agreement: they considered — and they were right — that I should agree with my Right Honourable Friend the Secretary of State for Trade and Industry that the fact that the then Defence Secretary's letter of the 3rd January was thought by the Solicitor-General to contain material inaccuracies which needed to be corrected should become public knowledge as soon as possible.' (23 Jan. c. 450). Nowhere do you say what led your office to consider that you would agree to the matter becoming public knowledge and in particular that you would agree to the fact that it was the Solicitor-General's opinion becoming public knowledge.

8. Equally, the then Secretary of State for Trade and Industry appears to have considered that you had consented. You say, 'He asked his officials to discuss with my office whether the disclosure should be made and, if so, whether it should be made from 10

Downing Street as he would prefer.' (23 Jan. c. 450).
You do not say what led the then Secretary of State
for Trade and Industry to suppose that the disclosure
might be made from 10 Downing Street, however
I note that you say, 'I discussed the matter with my
office the following day, when I also learned of the
Law Officer's concern. I was told that the Solicitor-
General's advice had not been disclosed by my
office.' (27 Jan. c. 657). It would appear, therefore,
that you also were under the impression that the
Solicitor-General's advice might have been disclosed
from your office.

9. Finally, you said, 'It was vital to have accurate
information in the public domain because we knew
that judgments might be founded on that . . .' (23
Jan. c. 455).

You did not say to whom you referred when you said 'we'
in the last passage quoted. Other than your goodself it may
include your officials, who knew your mind and through
whom you communicated with both the then Secretary of
State for Trade and Industry and the Solicitor-General. It
may include the then Secretary of State for Trade and
Industry, who contacted the Solicitor-General at your
request and who thought that the disclosure might be made
from 10 Downing Street. Finally, it might include the
person who reported the Solicitor-General's provisional
opinion to you; in that it was the Department of Trade and
Industry who first approached the Solicitor-General it
would follow that they also reported the outcome.
In any event, I am driven to conclude from your statement
and from your speech that the answer to my first question
is, 'Yes'. Should I be wrong in this conclusion I would be
grateful if you could disabuse me as soon as possible.
My second question was, 'When you agreed to the setting

up of an inquiry, did you at that stage know or have reason
to believe that it was an official leak?

In order to answer this question I have again referred to the
reports of your statement and of your speech, as you suggest.
I can find no passage where you expressly state that you did,
or that you did not, know or have reason to believe that the
'leak' was 'official' when you authorised the inquiry. I note
that you said, 'I did not know about the then Secretary of
State for Trade and Industry's own role in the matter of
the disclosure until the inquiry had reported.' (27 Jan. c.
657), however, with respect, I do not consider that statement to fully answer the question and I would be grateful
if you could draw my attention to any other passage which
might be of assistance to me.

I do not consider the above statement to fully answer the
question for the following reasons:

   1. You say, many times, in your statement and in
      your speech that the inquiry was set up to establish
      the facts. You further say, 'I did not know all the
      facts, . . .' (23 Jan. c. 453) and that 'many' (23 Jan.
      c. 453), 'an enormous number' (23 Jan. c. 454),
      'most' (23 Jan. cc. 455, 460) and 'a vast number'
      (23 Jan. c. 456) of the facts reported by the inquiry
      were not known to you until the 22nd January
      when the inquiry reported. You will appreciate,
      however, that non-specific statements as to what
      you *did not* know until the 22nd January do not
      answer the specific question as to what you *did* know
      on the 13th January when you authorised the inquiry.

   2. In seeking to discover, from your speech and your
      statement, what you did know on the 13th January
      we find that you learned about the disclosure of the
      Solicitor-General's letter 'some hours after it had
      occurred.' (27 Jan. c. 657) i.e. in the evening of the
      6th January. You say, 'I discussed the matter with

my office the following day, when I also learned of
the Law Officer's concern. I was told that the Solicitor-General's advice had not been disclosed by
my office. I was also told, in general terms, that
there had been contacts between my office and the
Department of Trade and Industry.' (27 Jan. c.
657).

3. You do not say what is meant by the phrase 'in
general terms' in this passage, however in that it is
there at all I infer that you were told more than the
mere fact that there had been contacts. The state of
your office's knowledge may be seen from the following passage: 'Officials in the Department of Trade
and Industry approached officials in my office, who
made it clear that it was not intended to disclose
the Solicitor-General's letter from 10 Downing
Street; but, being told that the Secretary of State
for Trade and Industry had authorised the disclosure,
they accepted that the Department of Trade and
Industry should make it and they accepted the
means by which it was proposed that the disclosure
should be made.' (27 Jan. c. 655). The extent to
which this knowledge is included under the head of
'general terms' is a matter for conjecture.

4. Further, you say, with reference to your statement
of the 23rd January, '. . . I set out the steps by
which the Solicitor-General's letter of 6 January was
made public, as this emerged both from the accounts
of officials as reported by the inquiry and also from
my subsequent discussions with the then Secretary
of State for Trade and Industry, . . .' (27 Jan. c.
654). A careful reading of this passage reveals that it
refers to discussions with the then Secretary of
State for Trade and Industry 'subsequent to the 6th
January'.

5. I conclude from the above that when your 'authority
was conveyed to the head of the Civil Service on
Monday 13 January' (27 Jan. c. 653) you had—

(a) been informed that the Law Officers considered that there should be an inquiry;

(b) discussed the matter with your office, who
were aware of the official nature of the
'leak', in general terms; and

(c) had discussions with the then Secretary of
State for Trade and Industry.

In the light of the above the inference can be drawn that,
at the time you authorised the inquiry, you knew or had
reason to believe that the disclosure was, in some way,
official. With respect I consider that, without further clarification, the statement that you 'did not know about the
then Secretary of State for Trade and Industry's own role in
the matter of the disclosure until the inquiry had reported.'
(27 Jan. c. 657) fails to deny this inference.

I would be grateful, therefore, if you could explain what is
meant by—

(a) 'General terms' (27 Jan. c. 657), stating
what terms were used and what information
was conveyed;

(b) 'Subsequent discussions' (27 Jan. c. 654)
stating what discussion you, or your Private
Secretary on your behalf, had with the then
Secretary of State for Trade and Industry
subsequent to the disclosure on the 6th January and before the 13th January;

(c) 'The then Secretary of State for Trade and
Industry's own role' (27 Jan. c. 657) stating
what is meant by the term 'role'.

In the absence of such clarification I must conclude from
your statement and from your speech that the answer to
my second question is also 'Yes'. Should I be wrong in so

concluding perhaps you would let me know.
I would be grateful if you could give these matters your
urgent attention.

Yours sincerely,

John Morris Q.C., M.P.

1O DOWNING STREET

THE PRIME MINISTER   10 March 1986

Dear Mr Morris,

Thank you for your further letter of 4 March in response
to mine of 24 February. The conclusions you draw from
our correspondence are entirely a matter for you. For my
part, I can only repeat that I gave a full account of the
circumstances of the disclosure of the Solicitor General's
letter of 6 January to the then Secretary of State for
Defence in my statement to the House on 23 January and
subsequently in the debate on 27 January. That account
was checked for accuracy with all those involved. I have
nothing to add to those statements.

Yours sincerely,

Margaret Thatcher

Index